A Teacher is a Special Person!

Compiled by Dr. Bernard E. Farber

Illustrations by Jenny Faw, Design by Andrew Faw

PETER PAUPER PRESS, INC.
WHITE PLAINS, NEW YORK

To my grandchildren,
Lauren, Sarah, Dena, and Nicole,
with love.

Copyright ©1996
Peter Pauper Press, Inc.
202 Mamaroneck Avenue
White Plains, NY 10601
ISBN 0-88088-686-2
Printed in China
7   6   5   4

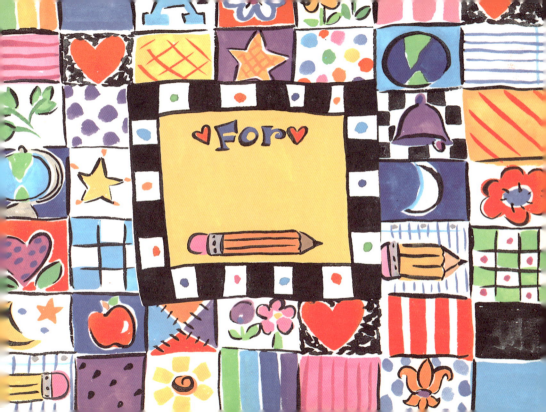

Introduction

A teacher is a special person. "A teacher affects eternity," Henry Adams stated, by shaping a child's intellectual and emotional view of himself and his surroundings. In turn, this vision affects the futures of both the child and those who will later touch his life.

A teacher's job is not an easy one. For a teacher to reach each child, and at the same time hold a class from scattering into dozens of fragments, requires an arsenal of skills, a character actor's range of roles, and the patience of several well-worn saints.

It is unlikely that at the end of each (or any) school day the students will rise up as one to say, "Thank you for teaching me today." It would be a rare moment for even one student to do so. So, rather than wait for a confluence of unlikely events, we have collected a book full of thoughts, observations, and declarations that, when compounded into one well-wrought sentence, sounds like this: "You, dear teacher, are a special person!"

THE EDITORS

A load of books does not equal one good teacher.

CHINESE PROVERB

I wish she was smart enough to teach second grade too, next year.

WILLIAM GOUMAS,
FIRST GRADE PUPIL, "FAVORITE TEACHER" ESSAY

*T*o teach is to learn twice over.

JOSEPH JOUBERT

*T*he art of teaching consists in helping students feel that although you may stand in front of them, you're really behind them.

ANONYMOUS

I have learned much from my teachers, and from my colleagues more than from my teachers, but from my disciples more than from them all.

TALMUD

*I*t is the supreme art of the teacher to awaken joy in creative expression and knowledge.

ALBERT EINSTEIN,
MOTTO FOR THE ASTRONOMY BUILDING, PASADENA JUNIOR COLLEGE

I'd like to learn a lot of things;
With curiosity I'm cursed.
But Teacher tells me that I must
Complete my education first.

ANONYMOUS

*I*f the heavens were all parchment, and the trees of the forest all pens, and every human being were a scribe, it would be impossible to record all that I have learned from my teachers.

ATTRIBUTED TO JOHANAN BEN ZAKKAI

*I*f I can teach you something, it may mean that I can count at least somewhere.

HANNAH GREEN,
I NEVER PROMISED YOU A ROSE GARDEN

*S*he used to be a schoolteacher but she has no class now.

FRED ALLEN

I'm not a teacher: only a fellow-traveller of whom you asked the way.
I pointed ahead—ahead of myself as well as of you.

GEORGE BERNARD SHAW

*G*ood teachers are costly, but bad teachers cost more.

BOB TALBERT

A successful teacher needs the education of a college president, the executive ability of a financier, the humility of a deacon, the adaptability of a chameleon, the hope of an optimist, the courage of a hero, the wisdom of a serpent, the gentleness of a dove, the patience of Job, the grace of God, and the persistence of the Devil.

ANONYMOUS

*T*he child is not there for you, but you are there for the child.

Samuel Raphael Hirsch

14

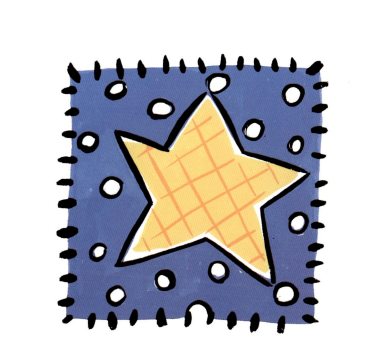

I have never heard anyone whom I consider a good teacher claim that he or she is a good teacher—in the way that one might claim to be a good writer or surgeon or athlete. Self-doubt seems very much a part of the job of teaching: one can never be sure how well it is going.

JOSEPH EPSTEIN

*N*o one should teach who is not a bit awed by the importance of the profession.

GEORGE E. FRASIER

*W*hat constitutes the teacher is the passion to make scholars.

GEORGE HERBERT PALMER

A teacher affects eternity; he can never tell where
his influence stops.

HENRY ADAMS,
THE EDUCATION OF HENRY ADAMS

I am quite sure that in the hereafter she will take me by the hand and lead me to my proper seat.

BERNARD BARUCH,
RECALLING ONE OF HIS EARLY TEACHERS

*A*nd when I am forgotten, as I shall be,
And asleep in dull cold marble, where no mention
Of me must be heard of, say, I taught thee.

WILLIAM SHAKESPEARE,
HENRY VIII

WORLD'S BEST TEACHER

*I*f the teacher is not respected,
And the students not cared for,
Confusion will arise, however clever one is.

LAO-TSE

*I*f you want to pick up a child from the ground you first have to bend down to him. If you don't, how will you reach him?

ABRAHAM CAHAN

*O*ne might as well say he has sold when no one has bought as to say he has taught when no one has learned.

JOHN DEWEY

*T*he things taught in colleges and schools are not an education, but the means of education.

RALPH WALDO EMERSON

*I*n school we add, multiply, and subtract,
Sometimes teachers don't like the way we act.
But if we are nice to them,
They'll be nice to you.
For it all depends
On who is nice to who.

ANONYMOUS STUDENT,
AGE EIGHT

*T*eaching is, in one of its aspects, a performing art.

JOSEPH EPSTEIN

*T*he important thing is not so much that every child should be taught as that every child should be given the wish to learn.

SIR JOHN LUBBOCK

*O*ne of the most important things a teacher can do is to send the pupil home in the afternoon liking himself just a little better than when he came in in the morning.

ERNEST MELBY,
QUOTED BY EDA LESHAN

*E*ducation must have an end in view, for it is not an end in itself.

SYBIL MARSHALL

*I*f you plan for a year, plant a seed. If for ten years, plant a tree. If for a hundred years, teach the people. When you sow a seed once, you will reap a single harvest. When you teach people, you will reap a hundred harvests.

KUAN CHUNG

*Y*ou don't have to talk too hard when you talk to a teacher.

J. D. Salinger,
The Catcher in the Rye

*I*f he is indeed wise he does not bid you enter the house of his wisdom, but rather leads you to the threshold of your own mind.

Kahlil Gibran,
The Prophet

*B*itter are the tears of a child:
  Sweeten them.
Deep are the thoughts of a child:
  Quiet them.
Sharp is the grief of a child:
  Take it from him.
Soft is the heart of a child:
  Do not harden it.
    LADY PAMELA WYNDHAM GLENCONNER

31

Stick to one simple rule: "Tell 'em what you're gonna learn 'em; then learn 'em; then ask 'em: 'What did I just learn you?'"

SAM LEVENSON,
YOU DON'T HAVE TO BE IN WHO'S WHO TO KNOW WHAT'S WHAT

*T*he first duty of a lecturer—to hand you after an hour's discourse a nugget of pure truth to wrap up between the pages of your notebooks and keep on your mantlepiece forever.

VIRGINIA WOOLF,
A ROOM OF ONE'S OWN

"*C*an't you simplify the course?" the parent asked. "My child will never take all that in. She wants to get through by a shorter route."

"Certainly," answered the teacher, "I can arrange that. It depends of course, on what you want to make of her. When God wants an oak, it takes a hundred years, but when God wants to make a squash, it requires only two months."

PARAPHRASED FROM JAMES A. GARFIELD

*W*hen I transfer my knowledge, I teach. When I transfer my beliefs, I indoctrinate.

ARTHUR DANTO

*F*or every person wishing to teach there are thirty not wanting to be taught.

W. C. SELLAR AND R. J. YEATMAN

*W*e cannot form our children as we would wish; as God has given us them, so we must accept and love, educate them as we best may, and rest content. For each has different gifts; every one is useful, but in its proper way.

JOHANN WOLFGANG VON GOETHE

*I*f education doesn't prepare the young to educate themselves throughout their lives, then it is a failure, no matter what else it may seem to accomplish.

SYDNEY J. HARRIS

*W*e teachers can only help the work going on . . .

MARIA MONTESSORI,
THE ABSORBENT MIND

*T*he object of teaching a child is to enable him to get along without
his teacher.

ELBERT HUBBARD

I'd rather see a lesson than hear one any day;
I'd rather one should walk with me than merely show the way.
The eye's a better pupil and more willing than the ear;
Fine counsel is confusing, but example always clear.

ANONYMOUS,
TO MY TEACHER

*T*eaching kids to count is fine, but teaching them what counts is best.

*F*irst teach a person to develop to the point of his limitations and then—pfft!—break the limitation.

VIOLA SPOLIN

*E*ducation don't come by bumping against the schoolhouse.

AFRICAN-AMERICAN PROVERB

*T*each as though you were teaching your own children.

ANONYMOUS

*E*ducation is to get where you can start to learn.

GEORGE AIKEN

*L*earning . . .should be a joy and full of excitement. It is life's greatest adventure; it is an illustrated excursion into the mind of noble and learned men, not a conducted tour through a jail.

TAYLOR CALDWELL

*E*ducation is learning what you didn't know you didn't know.

Daniel J. Boorstin

*P*ersonally I'm always ready to learn, although I do not always like being taught.

Winston Churchill

*E*ducation is that which remains, if one has forgotten everything he learned in school.

ALBERT EINSTEIN

*G*ood teaching is one-fourth preparation and three-fourths theatre.

GAIL GODWIN

49

*I*f you promise not to believe everything your child says happens at this school, I'll promise not to believe everything he says happens at home.

ENGLISH SCHOOLMASTER,
NOTE TO PARENTS

*S*poon feeding in the long run teaches us nothing but the shape of the spoon.

E. M. FORSTER

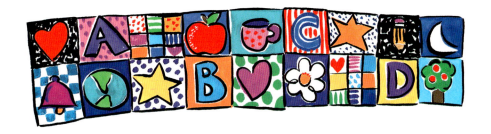

*E*ducation is the ability to listen to almost anything without losing your temper or your self-confidence.

ROBERT FROST

*T*he real menace in dealing with a five-year-old is that in no time at all you begin to sound like a five-year-old.

JEAN KERR,
PLEASE DON'T EAT THE DAISIES

*"B*ut we don't want to teach 'em," replied the Badger. "We want to learn 'em."

KENNETH GRAHAME,
THE WIND IN THE WILLOWS

*T*he only reason I always try to meet and know the parents better is because it helps me to forgive their children.

LOUIS JOHANNOT

*H*e had a way of meeting a simple question with a compound answer—you could take the part you wanted, and leave the rest.

Eva Lathbury

I touch the future. I teach.

Christa McAuliffe

*T*he best and briefest reason for a good education is that the more effort you expend in sharpening the ax, the less effort you have to expend in chopping the wood.

SYDNEY J. HARRIS

*E*ducation costs money, but then so does ignorance.

*S*IR *C*LAUS *M*OSER

*T*eachers can change lives with just the right mix of chalk and challenges.

*J*OYCE *A*. *M*YERS

*W*hat a teacher doesn't say . . . is a telling part of what a student hears.

MAURICE NATANSON

*T*o reach a child's mind a teacher must capture his heart. Only if a child feels right can he think right.

HAIM G. GINNOTT

Some days we play with clay.
Some days we don't.
I'd like to play with clay today.
But teacher says we won't.

JUDY LYNN STEWART,
GRADE 3

60

*T*he most important part of teaching = to teach what it is to *know*.

SIMONE WEIL

*L*earning stamps you with its moments. Childhood's learning is made up of moments. It isn't steady. It's a pulse.

Eudora Welty,
One Writer's Beginning

I'm never going to be a movie star. But then, in all probability, Liz Taylor is never going to teach first and second grade.

Mary J. Wilson

*G*oodbye tension, hello pension!

FAY MICHAUD,
RETIRING TEACHER